995

tion.

For 50. more - -

Love, 😊

The Sound of Water

古池や蛙とびこむ水の音

花咣

THE
SOUND
OF WATER

Haiku by Bashō, Buson,
Issa, and Other Poets

Translated by Sam Hamill
Illustrated by Kaji Aso

SHAMBHALA
Boston & London
1995

Shambhala Publications, Inc.
Horticultural Hall
300 Massachusetts Avenue
Boston, Massachusetts 02115

9 8 7 6 5 4 3 2 1

First Edition
Printed in the United States of America on acid-free paper ⊗
Distributed in the United States by Random House, Inc.,
and in Canada by Random House of Canada Ltd

Library of Congress Cataloging-in-Publication Data
The sound of water: haiku by Bashō, Buson, Issa, and other
    poets / translated by Sam Hamill.
        p.   cm.—(Shambhala centaur editions)
    ISBN 1-57062-019-9
        1. Haiku—Translations into English.   2. Japanese
poetry—Edo period, 1600–1868—Translations into
English.   I. Hamill, Sam.   II. Series.
PL782.E3S65   1994   94-7609
895.6'104—dc20   CIP

for

Eron Hamill

and Gray Foster

and Galen Garwood

Contents

Translator's Introduction

"Haiku," Bashō (1644–1694) was fond of saying, "is the heart of the *Man'yoshu*," the first imperial anthology, compiled in the eighth century. "Haiku," many modern Japanese poets are fond of saying, "began and ended with Bashō." Look beyond the hyperbole of either observation, and there is a powerful element of truth. As one Japanese poet told me, "There's only Bashō—and Buson and Issa are, as you say, exceptions proving the rule."

In three lines totalling seventeen syllables measuring 5-7-5, a great haiku presents—

through imagery drawn from intensely careful observation—a web of associated ideas (*rensō*) requiring an active mind on the part of the listener. When Bashō writes:

> How reluctantly
> the bee emerges from deep
> within the peony

is he merely presenting a pathetical fallacy, attributing human emotion to a bee, or is he entering into the authentic experience of "beeness" as deeply as possible? Perhaps both qualities are present. His detailed observation calls for something other than metaphor; it demands literal accuracy. Is the bee inside his mind or outside? The poem moves in part because of tension raised through the underlying question of duality that Zen resolves in silence.

The bee, the peony, the poet—all one idea composed of many.

In another poem, Bashō finds

> Delight, then sorrow,
> aboard the cormorant
> fishing boat

without having to describe for his audience the nooses tied around the throats of fishing birds to inhibit swallowing. He is initially delighted by their amazing skill and grace, then horrified that they cannot swallow what they catch, saddened by their captivity and exploitation, and perhaps even more deeply saddened by the fishingfolk he never mentions. What remains unstated begs for a profound moral equation, although only the poet's compassion is clearly implied.

The best haiku reflect an undeniable Zen influence. Elements of compassion, silence, and awareness of temporality often combine to reveal a sense of mystery. Just as often, haiku may bring a startling insight into the ordinary, as when Buson writes:

> Nobly, the great priest
> deposits his daily stool
> in bleak winter fields

thereby reminding his audience that nobility has nothing whatever to do with palaces and embroidered robes, but that true nobility is obtainable in *every* human endeavor.

Issa reminds the attentive listener:

> A world of dew,
> and within every dewdrop
> a world of struggle

Haiku may be the most widely recognizable poetic form in the world. At play with the form, children quickly discover their own poetic imaginations; almost anyone can learn to make decently readable haiku in no time at all. Just as anyone can learn to write a quatrain or a sonnet. The problem remains: to be great, a poem must rise on its own merit, and too much haiku is merely haiku. Haiku written in American English and attempting to borrow traditional Japanese literary devices usually ends up smelling of the bric-a-brac shop, all fragmentary dust and mold or cheap glitter coating the ordinary, or—worse—the merely cute or contrived. Great haiku cuts both ways, sometimes witty or sarcastic, sometimes making Zenlike demands for that most extraordinary consciousness, no-mind or ordinary-mind.

Haiku should be approached with a daily sort of reverence, as we might approach an encounter with a great spiritual teacher. It is easy to imitate; it is difficult to attain. The more deeply the reader enters into the authentic experience of the poem, the more the poem reveals. When Kikaku writes,

> In the Emperor's bed,
> the smell of burnt mosquitoes,
> and erotic whispers

we must realize first that the burning of mosquitoes clears the air for erotic play; then we may wonder whether the "smell of burnt mosquitoes" might become a kind of erotic incense for the Emperor, a stimulant for his lust. Thus, lust, love and death are joined in primal experience. Is there a buried needle in this verse? Does Kikaku intend for us to think critically of a decadent emperor? And what does that reveal about ourselves? Revealing the relationship between these mundane activities shakes up our polite perceptions like a Zen slap in the face—a call to awaken to what actually is.

Haiku, sprung free from the opening lines of predominantly humorous "linked verse" (*renga*) created by multiple authors, began to articulate aesthetic qualities such as a sense of beautiful aloneness, *sabishisa*, and restrained elegance, *furyu*.

Bashō brought to haiku "the Way of Elegance" (*fuga-no-michi*), deepened its Zen influence, and approached poetry itself as a way of life (*kadō*, the way of poetry) in the belief that poetry could be a source of enlightenment. "Achieve enlightenment, then return to this world of ordinary humanity," he advised. And, "Do not follow in the footsteps of the old masters, but seek what they sought." His "way of elegance" did not include the mere trappings associated with elegance; he sought the authentic vision of "the ancients."

Born into a samurai family prominent among nobility, Bashō rejected that world and became a wanderer, studying Zen, history, and classical Chinese poetry, living in apparently blissful poverty under a modest patronage and from donations by his many students. In addition to being the supreme artist of haiku and renga, Bashō wrote *haibun*, brief prose-and-poetry travelogues like *Narrow Road to the Interior*, that are absolutely nonpareil in the literature of the world.

If Bashō is the great river of haiku, Buson and Issa are primary tributaries. If Bashō lived and advocated a life of solitary poverty and travel, Buson (1715–1783), by contrast, appears to have been a devoted family man and a successful painter. While he "sought what Bashō sought," he did not share his master's rigorous Zen discipline nor his deep classicism. Buson's major contribution to haiku is his complexity and his painter's eye. Whereas Bashō taught, "Master technique, then forget it," Buson's technique is less transparent, his poems more consciously composed. He is a poet of enhanced sensibility and evocation.

Issa (1762–1826) wrote poetry that is especially remarkable considering the life of the poet. His mother died while he was an infant, and his stepmother was a plague upon his soul until he left home at fourteen. He lived in poverty for twenty years before returning for his father's death in 1801. Although he was named principal heir in his father's will, his stepmother and half brother conspired successfully to keep Issa from the property for thirteen more years. He would eventually write:

> My dear old village,
> every memory of home
> pierces like a thorn

When he finally returned from Edo (Tokyo), he married a young village woman, but all five of their children died, as did his wife of ten years. And his house burned down. He lived four more years, married again, and finally had an heir, a baby girl—born shortly after his death.

Neither as at ease as Bashō nor as composed as Buson, Issa wrote a more personal poetry, moving steadily into a Pure Land Buddhist philosophy that expressed true devotion without getting caught up in the snares of mere religious dogmatism. Sometimes humorous or sarcastic, often of uneven quality, his poems are prized for their remarkably compassionate and poignant insight. Following the death of one of his children, he wrote:

> This world of dew
> is only a world of dew—
> and yet

And the poem is large enough—and sufficiently particular—to say it all. As is so often the case, the most important part is that which is left unstated.

The great age of haiku spans only a little over a hundred years, and yet its poetry is a river that continues to flow. In our own age and language, wonderful haiku have been written by poets as diverse as Gary Snyder, Richard Wright, Lew Welch, and Richard Wilbur, to name but a few.

Bashō is neither the beginning nor the end. Re-encountering these poems and translating them has been, like the leap of Bashō's famous frog, a plunge into the sound of water, each brief poem expanding in ever-widening ripples.

Sam Hamill
Port Townsend, Washington
1993

Bashō

ねむる蝶、

何を

夢みて

羽根づかい

花兄

How very noble!
One who finds no satori
in the lightning-flash

Breakfast enjoyed
in the fine company of
morning glories

Traveling this high
mountain trail, delighted
by violets

A solitary
crow on a bare branch—
autumn evening

This first fallen snow
is barely enough to bend
the jonquil leaves

Whore and monk, we sleep
under one roof together,
moon in a field of clover

At the ancient pond
a frog plunges into
the sound of water

Now I see her face,
the old woman, abandoned,
the moon her only companion

Nothing in the cry
of cicadas suggests they
are about to die

How reluctantly
the bee emerges from deep
within the peony

The farmer's roadside
hedge provided lunch for
my tired horse

How wild the sea is,
and over Sado Island,
the River of Heaven

Seen in plain daylight
the firefly's nothing but
an insect

Delight, then sorrow,
aboard the cormorant
fishing boat

Exhausted, I sought
a country inn, but found
wisteria in bloom

Among moon gazers
at the ancient temple grounds
not one beautiful face

A cuckoo cries,
and through a thicket of bamboo
the late moon shines

This hot day swept away
into the sea by the
Mogami River

All along this road
not a single soul—only
autumn evening comes

Heard, not seen,
the camellia poured rainwater
when it leaned

The banana tree
blown by winds pours raindrops
into the bucket

With plum blossom scent,
this sudden sun emerges
along a mountain trail

Lead my pony
across this wide moor to where
the cuckoo sings

Wrapping dumplings in
bamboo leaves, with one finger
she tidies her hair

With a warbler for
a soul, it sleeps peacefully,
this mountain willow

This dark autumn
old age settles down on me
like heavy clouds or birds

The morning glories
bloom, securing the gate
in the old fence

From every direction
cherry blossom petals blow
into Lake Biwa

Long conversations
beside blooming irises—
joys of life on the road

On Buddha's birthday
a spotted fawn is born—
just like that

On Buddha's deathday,
wrinkled tough old hands pray—
the prayer beads' sound

Behind Ise Shrine,
unseen, hidden by the fence,
Buddha enters nirvana

This ruined temple
should have its sad tale told only
by the clam digger

Autumnal full moon,
the tides slosh and foam
coming in

Crossing half the sky,
on my way to the capital,
big clouds promise snow

Gray hairs being plucked,
and from below my pillow
a cricket singing

Searching storehouse eaves,
rapt in plum blossom smells,
the mosquito hums

Polished and polished
clean, in the holy mirror
snow flowers bloom

Along my journey
through this transitory world,
new year's housecleaning

Through frozen rice fields,
moving slowly on horseback,
my shadow creeps by

The warbler sings
among new shoots of bamboo
of coming old age

A lovely spring night
suddenly vanished while we
viewed cherry blossoms

Come out to view
the truth of flowers blooming
in poverty

Autumn approaches
and the heart begins to dream
of four-tatami rooms

Winter showers,
even the monkey searches
for a raincoat

A weathered skeleton
in windy fields of memory,
piercing like a knife

Chilling autumn rains
curtain Mount Fuji, then make it
more beautiful to see

With dewdrops dripping,
I wish somehow I could wash
this perishing world

Seas slowly darken
and the wild duck's plaintive cry
grows faintly white

Water-drawing rites,
icy sound of monks' *getas*
echo long and cold

Getas are wooden-soled sandals.

That great blue oak
indifferent to all blossoms
appears more noble

The clouds come and go,
providing a rest for all
the moon viewers

Kannon's tiled temple
roof floats far away in clouds
of cherry blossoms

This bright harvest moon
keeps me walking all night long
around the little pond

Kannon is the Bodhisattva of Compassion.

Awakened at midnight
by the sound of the water jar
cracking from the ice

Clouds of cherry blossoms!
Is that temple bell in Ueno
or Asakusa?

Even these long days
are not nearly long enough
for the skylarks to sing

I'm a wanderer
so let that be my name—
the first winter rain

Summer grasses:
all that remains of great soldiers'
imperial dreams

From all these trees—
in salads, soups, everywhere—
cherry blossoms fall

Culture's beginnings:
rice-planting songs from the heart
of the country

Singing, planting rice,
village songs more lovely
than famous city poems

All the field hands
enjoy a noontime nap after
the harvest moon

Winter seclusion—
sitting propped against
the same worn post

I would like to use
that scarecrow's tattered clothes
in this midnight frost

Lonely silence,
a single cicada's cry
sinking into stone

But for a woodpecker
tapping at a post, no sound
at all in the house

Ungraciously, under
a great soldier's empty helmet,
a cricket sings

Wet with morning dew
and splotched with mud, the melon
looks especially cool

Even in Kyoto,
how I long for Kyoto
when the cuckoo sings

Your song caresses
the depth of loneliness,
O high mountain bird

Tremble, oh my gravemound,
in time my cries will be
only this autumn wind

On New Year's Day
each thought a loneliness
as winter dusk descends

BASHŌ'S DEATH POEM

Sick on my journey,
only my dreams will wander
these desolate moors

Buson

春の海
ひねもす
のたり
のたり哉

花光

New Year's first poem
written, now self-satisfied,
O haiku poet!

A lightning flash—
the sound of water drops
falling through bamboo

With a woman friend,
bowing at the Great Palace—
a pale, hazy moon

Rain falls on the grass,
filling the ruts left by
the festival cart

Priestly poverty—
he carves a wooden buddha
through a long cold night

At the ancient well,
leaping high for mosquitos,
that fish-dark sound

I go out alone
to visit a man alone
in this autumn dusk

Moon in midsky, high
over the village hovels
and wandering on

Goodbye. I will go
alone down Kiso Road
old as autumn

With no underrobes,
bare butt suddenly exposed—
a gust of spring wind

Sweet springtime showers
and no words can express
how sad it all is

With a runny nose
sitting alone at the Go board,
a long cold night

On these southern roads,
on shrine or thatched roof, all the same,
swallows everywhere

An evening cloudburst—
sparrows cling desperately
to trembling bushes

At a roadside shrine,
before the stony buddha
a firefly burns

These lazy spring days
continue—but how far away
those times called Long Ago!

A long hard journey,
rain beating down the clover
like a wanderer's feet

The late evening crow
of deep autumn longing
suddenly cries out

In a bitter wind
a solitary monk bends
to words cut in stone

Nobly, the great priest
deposits his daily stool
in bleak winter fields

Walking on dishes
the rat's feet make the music
of shivering cold

Utter aloneness—
another great pleasure
in autumn twilight

The *thwack* of an ax
in the heart of a thicket—
and woodpecker's *tat-tats!*

With the noon conch blown
those old rice-planting songs
are suddenly gone

This cold winter night,
that old wooden-head buddha
would make a nice fire

The ferry departs
as the tardy man stands in
the first winter rain

Not cherry blossoms
but peach blossom sweetness
surrounds this little house

By flowering pear
and by the lamp of the moon
she reads her letter

Autumn breezes
spin small fish hung to dry
from beach house eaves

Head pillowed on arm,
such affection for myself!
and this smoky moon

Clinging to the bell
he dozes so peacefully,
this new butterfly

Fallen red blossoms
from plum trees burst into flame
among the horse turds

Light winter rain
like scampering rat's-feet
over my koto

Bamboo hat, straw coat—
the very essence of Bashō—
falling winter rain

Koto is a traditional Japanese stringed musical
instrument.

A flying squirrel
munches a small bird's bones
in a bare winter field

Along the roadside
discarded duckweed blossoms
in the evening rain

In seasonal rain
along a nameless river
fear too has no name

Pure white plum blossoms
slowly begin to turn
the color of dawn

Plum blossoms in bloom,
in a Kitano teahouse,
the master of sumo

Only the shoots
of new green leaves, white water,
and yellow barley

In pale moonlight
the wisteria's scent
comes from far away

Slung over a screen,
a dress of silk and gauze.
The autumn wind.

The camellia tips,
the remains of last night's rain
splashing out

When a heavy cart
comes rumbling along
peonies tremble

That handsaw marks time
with the sound of poverty
late on a winter night

Darting here and there,
the bat is exploring
the moonlit plum

On the Anniversary of the Death of Bashō

Winter rain on moss
soundlessly recalls those
happy bygone days

Issa

Thus spring begins: old
stupidities repeated,
new errs invented

Just beyond the gate,
a neat yellow hole—
someone pissed in the snow

With this rising bath-mist
deep in a moonlit night,
spring finally begins.

People working fields,
from my deepest heart, I bow.
Now a little nap.

In the beggar's tin
a few thin copper coins
and this evening rain

For you too, my fleas,
the night passes so slowly.
But you won't be lonely.

Brilliant moon,
is it true that you too
must pass in a hurry

The winter fly
I caught and finally freed
the cat quickly ate

A faint yellow rose
almost hidden in deep grass—
and then it moves.

Mother, I weep
for you as I watch the sea
each time I watch the sea

As the great old trees
are marked for felling, the birds
build their new spring nests

Like misty moonlight,
watery, bewildering—
our temporal way

My dear old village,
every memory of home
pierces like a thorn

A sheet of rain.
Only one man remains among
cherry blossom shadows

A flowering plum
and a nightingale's love song—
he remains alone

My old village lies
far beyond what we can see,
but there the lark is singing

This world of dew
is only a world of dew—
and yet

Here in Shinano
are famous moons, and buddhas,
and our good noodles

When the wild turnip
burst into full blossom
a skylark sang

The distant mountains
are reflected in the eye
of the dragonfly

What's the lord's vast wealth
to me, his millions and more?
Dew on trembling grass

Before this autumn wind
even the shadows of mountains
shudder and tremble

This year on, forever,
it's all gravy for me now—
now spring arrives

I wish she were here
to listen to my bitching
and enjoy this moon

Gratitude for gifts,
even snow on my bedspread
a gift from the Pure Land

The old dog listens
intently, as if to the
worksongs of the worms

My spring is just this:
a single bamboo shoot,
a willow branch

From that woman
on the beach, dusk pours out
across the evening waves

Don't kill that poor fly!
He cowers, wringing
his hands for mercy

Before I arrived,
who were the people living here?
Only violets remain.

O autumn winds,
tell me where I'm bound, to which
particular hell

From the Great Buddha's
great nose, a swallow comes
gliding out

A world of dew,
and within every dewdrop
a world of struggle

Under this bright moon
I sit like an old buddha
knees spread wide

The young sparrows
return into Jizō's sleeve
for sanctuary

My noontime nap
disrupted by voices singing
rice-planting songs

Jizō is the patron bodhisattva of children
and travelers.

In the midst of this world
we stroll along the roof of hell
gawking at flowers

Give me a homeland,
and a passionate woman,
and winter alone

A world of trials,
and if the cherry blossoms,
it simply blossoms

In my hidden house,
no teeth left in the mouth,
but good luck abounds

So many flea bites,
but on her lovely young skin
they are beautiful

Now we are leaving,
the houseflies can make love
to their hearts' desire

The new year arrived
in utter simplicity—
and a deep blue sky

The blossoming plum!
Today all the fires of hell
remain empty

Just to say the word
home, that one word alone,
so pleasantly cool

How comfortable
my summer cotton robe
when drenched with sweat

In this mountain village,
shining in my soup bowl,
the bright moon arrives

After a long nap,
the cat yawns, rises, and goes out
looking for love

O summer snail,
you climb but slowly, slowly
to the top of Fuji

The vanity of men—
they would like to retain
this passing winter moon

Other Poets

春の海　ひねもす　のたり　のたり　かな

蕪村

MORITAKE [1452–1540]

Those falling blossoms
all return to the branch when
I watch butterflies

SŌIN [1604–1682]

Settling, white dew
does not discriminate,
each drop its home

ANONYMOUS

Chanting Buddha's name
is the deepest pleasure
of one's old age

To learn how to die
watch cherry blossoms, observe
chrysanthemums

SANPŪ [1647–1732]

First cherry blossoms,
a cuckoo, the moon and snow:
another year closes

KIKAKU [1661–1707]

O Great Buddha,
your lap must be filling with
these flowers of snow

Her mate devoured
by the cat, the cricket's wife
must be mourning

On Buddha's birthday
the orphaned boy will become
the temple's child

In the Emperor's bed,
the smell of burnt mosquitoes,
and erotic whispers

A single yam leaf
contains the entire life
of a water drop

Over the long road
the flower-bringer follows:
plentiful moonlight

I begin each day
with breakfast greens and tea
and morning glories

Riding the wide leaf
of the banana-tree,
the tree-frog clings

RANSETSU [1654–1707]

A single leaf falls,
then suddenly another,
stolen by the breeze

A large slug slides
slowly, glistening over
abandoned armor

On the old plum tree,
one blossom by one blossom,
the spring thaw is born

All by itself,
that beautiful melon,
entirely self-sufficient

Without a sound,
munching young rice-plant stalks,
a caterpillar dines

KYORAI [1651–1704]

Returning from a funeral
I saw this very moon
high above the moor

RAIZAN [1653–1716]

For rice-planting women
there's nothing left unsoiled
but their song

KAKEI [d. 1716]

At the break of dawn
the well-bucket reels in
a camellia bloom

ONITSURA [1660–1738]

To finally know
the plum, use the whole heart too,
and your own nose

The leaping trout sees
far below, a few white clouds
as they flow

True obedience:
silently the flowers speak
to the inner ear

The cherry blossoms
scatter and we watch and then
more cherry blossoms blow

TAIGI [d. 1771]

"Don't touch!" my host cried,
then broke off and presented
a flowering plum

Chiyo [1701–1775]

Since morning glories
hold my well-bucket hostage,
I beg for water

Sogetsuni [d. ca. 1804]

After the Dance for the Dead
only pine winds to bring
these insect cries

Divine mystery
in these autumn leaves that fall
on stony buddhas

SOGI [1421–1502]

Life in this world
is brief as time spent sheltered
from winter showers

FUHAKU [1714–1807]

So very still, even
cherry blossoms are not stirred
by the temple bell

TEIGA [1744–1826]

In the poor man's house,
crossing the tatami mats,
a cold autumn wind

KIKUSHA-NI [1752–1826]

Only the moon
and I, on our meeting-bridge,
alone, growing cold

TAYO-JO [1772–1865]

People, more people
scurrying through spring breezes
along the rice-field dikes

SŌCHŌ [1448–1532]

The moon this evening,
and in the whole wide sky
not a trace of cloud

SHŌHA [19th century]

When the bush warbler
sings, the old frog belches
his reply

SHIKI [1867–1902]

Just when the sermon
has finally dirtied my ears—
the cuckoo

O autumn winds,
for me there are no ancient
gods, no buddhas for me

The Skylark School
argues with the Frog School,
each with its song

The full moon ringed
by these innumerable stars,
and the sky deep green

In the winter river,
discarded, an old dog's
carcass

The thunderstorm breaks up,
one tree lit by setting sun,
a cicada cry

SHAMBHALA CENTAUR EDITIONS are named for a classical modern typeface designed by the eminent American typographer Bruce Rogers. Modeled on a fifteenth-century Roman type, Centaur was originally an exclusive titling font for the Metropolitan Museum of Art, New York. The first book in which it appeared was Maurice de Guérin's *The Centaur*, printed in 1915. Until recently, Centaur type was available only for handset books printed on letter-press. Its elegance and clarity make it the typeface of choice for Shambhala Centaur Editions, which include outstanding classics of the world's literary and spiritual traditions.

SHAMBHALA CENTAUR EDITIONS

THE BOOK OF THE HEART
Embracing the Tao
    by Loy Ching-Yuen
        Translated by Trevor Carolan and Bella Chen

DEWDROPS ON A LOTUS LEAF
Zen Poems of Ryōkan
        Translated by John Stevens

DREAM CONVERSATIONS
On Buddhism and Zen
    by Musō Kokushi
        Translated by Thomas Cleary

FOR LOVE OF THE DARK ONE
Songs of Mirabai
        Translated by Andrew Schelling
        Illustrated by Mayumi Oda

FOUR HUTS
Asian Writings on the Simple Life
    Translated by Burton Watson

LOOK! THIS IS LOVE
Poems of Rumi
    Translated by Annemarie Schimmel

MIDNIGHT FLUTE
Chinese Poems of Love and Longing
    Translated by Sam Hamill

NARROW ROAD TO THE INTERIOR
    by Matsuo Bashō
    Translated by Sam Hamill

ONLY COMPANION
Japanese Poems of Love and Longing
    Translated by Sam Hamill

(Continued on next page)

PRAYER OF THE HEART
Writings from the Philokalia
Compiled by St. Nicodemus of the Holy
Mountain and St. Macarios of Corinth
Translated by G. E. H. Palmer, Philip Sherrard,
and Kallistos Ware

THE SOUND OF WATER
Haiku by Bashō, Buson, Issa, and Other Poets
Translated by Sam Hamill

A STRANGER TO HEAVEN AND EARTH
Poems of Anna Akhmatova
Translated by Judith Hemschemeyer

THE TALE OF CUPID & PSYCHE
by Lucius Apuleius
Translated by Robert Graves

A TOUCH OF GRACE
Songs of Kabir
Translated by Linda Hess and Shukdev Singh